TAMING
YOUR
INNER
SUPERVISOR

BOOK THREE

HIRING AND FIRING

h·a·a·g

environmental
press

by Ruth Haag

illustrated by Bob Haag

TAMING YOUR INNER SUPERVISOR   BOOK THREE   HIRING AND FIRING

Text and Illustration Copyright © 1999 by Ruth S. Haag

Published by haag environmental press

Printed in the United States of America
For information contact: Haag Environmental Press, 1064 N. Main St #401, Bowling Green, OH 43402-1346

Library of Congress Catalog Card Number: 99-94227

ISBN 0-9665497-2-4

to Bob

day after day
year after year
it just gets better

TABLE OF CONTENTS

PROLOG:

People respond to what you say, how you say it, and how you act. If you go to a store and are hostile and angry with the clerk, you will not receive very good service. If you accuse your teenagers of misbehaving, they will clam up and refuse to talk to you.

For supervisors, your employees respond to both the verbal messages you deliver, and the behavior which you use when you deliver them. If you never confront your employees when they make mistakes, they will continue to make them, and you will have to do their work for them. If you yell at your employees every time that you see them, they will begin to ignore you. If you demand that your employees serve you coffee and clean up behind you, they will resent you.

Much of learning to be a good supervisor is really learning to communicate properly with your employees. The great majority of supervisory problems have their roots in poor communication.

The way in which we communicate is dictated by our personality. Most supervisors fit into one of three supervisor personality categories. If the supervisor can learn to tame their personality, they will learn to communicate better with their employees.

A **sensitive supervisor** is afraid to confront their employees. They hope that if they ignore the problem, it will just go away. The sensitive supervisor has to learn to confront their employees, as near to the time of the transgression as possible.

The **belligerent supervisor** is often angry. They are frustrated with having to take the time to supervise anyone, and are angry when things go wrong. They want to find any employee to blame, yell at them and be done with it. The belligerent supervisor has to learn to stop and wait, sometimes as much as a day, before they confront their employees.

The **regal supervisor** is actually afraid of losing their own job. They see their employees as a threat to their position. They spend much of their time trying to make sure that they look supervisory. They tend to keep information from their employees so that they, the supervisor, can keep in control. They give out assignments piecemeal and check their employees often. The regal supervisor has to learn to give out enough information for their employees to work alone for up to two days. They have to fight their urge to look supervisory, and fight their fear of losing their job.

When a supervisor learns about their own personality, tames their behavior, and improves their communication skills, most employee performance problems will be solved. There are times, however, when none of these things work, because the employee is just not the right person for the job. Careful hiring practices can help to lessen the number of these types of problems. Nonetheless, ultimately, some employees will have to be fired.

Both hiring and firing need to be done with much thought and care. The goal of careful hiring is to find the best person for the job. The goal of firing is to remove a person who cannot do the job in a way which is as graceful and non-damaging as possible.

CHAPTER 1...HIRING: IS SCREENING PEOPLE REALLY NECESSARY?

A Story About Jim's Hiring System

Jim had been in business for one month. In addition to his job with his business, he was teaching part-time at a small local college. He knew that in the Summer he would need to expand his staff. He figured that college students were good workers, and his class was full of college students. So, one day, at the beginning of class Jim said:

"I have a business and will need some full-time and part-time help. Any of you who wants a job can have one, just stop by my office and fill out some employment papers."

Jim hired all of the students who came, just as he had promised. In total, seven students came, and one brought along another student from the same major, who had not been in Jim's class.

Jim suddenly had two problems. First, no matter how hard he tried, most of his new employees did not seem to understand the work and were not able to do it. Second, he had more students working than he had billable work to do. He had hired too many people.

Over the course of the next year, Jim had to fire half of his new employees, and was relieved when the other half quit.

Analysis: Interviews Are a Good Thing

The reason that Jim had such a dismal success rate was that he did not interview or carefully screen his new employees. He was using a system which he later named "everyone has a niche". He felt strongly that everyone could find a place to work in every company. Later, after this experience, he proclaimed that some people are "nicheless".

Jim actually knew very little about the people who he was hiring, he just figured you could hire everyone and then let things settle out. Had he gone through an interview process, he might not have hired <u>any</u> of these people.

Many employers determine that an interview is not necessary. They say things like:

"Our training is so rough that only the good people will make it through, so I hire everyone and let the training sort them out."

"I hire younger women, they will get pregnant and quit within a few years, so if it doesn't work out, I won't be stuck with them."

Some people claim to do a bit more screening:

"I just read the resumes and determine if they have the training and experience that I am looking for."

"I decide by how the person is dressed; pressed clothing, polished shoes, and I hire them."

All of these ideas carry a common thread, instead of a hiring decision being made about the particular person's ability to do the job, everyone is hired with the hope that they will work out somehow.

This "non-decision" system creates major supervisory management problems. These problems often take a long time to resolve.

CHAPTER 2...HIRING: SETTING HIRING GOALS

A Story About an Interview

Sally was ready to do her first interview. She had a list of questions to ask. She had had some difficulty coming up with questions, but felt she had come up with some good ones. The interviewee arrived and Sally escorted him to her office. She started through her list of questions:

"How did you find out about our company?"

"How many other jobs have you had related to this line of work?"

"Are you married?"

"Have you ever supervised anyone?"

"How much are you being paid now?"

She liked the candidate quite a bit. He was well dressed, and answered the questions promptly. Sally decided to offer him a job.

When Sally's first hire began to work, the technical supervisor came to see her.

"How did you let that Bozo slip through? He doesn't know the first thing about engineering, he has only an associate degree, we need someone with at least a bachelor's degree!"

Sally was mortified. She had obviously asked the wrong questions.

Analysis: You Must Set Hiring Goals

Before you begin the hiring process, you must determine what attributes you are looking for in an employee. Generally, you are looking for someone with a specific experience background. Also, you will be happiest with an employee who has the same basic work ethics as you do. It will be relatively easy to come up with relevant interview questions once you determine what your goals are:

- Do you want a person who will happily work extra hours, without complaint?

- Do you want a person who has many outside activities and interests, thus able to spread your company's exposure?

- Do you want a person who will follow the management's programs without complaint?

- Can you only respect a person who will take a stand and not ever back down, even if they get fired?

- Are you interested in someone with special training or skills?

- Are you interested in finding a person with a cheerful attitude?

- Are you interested in finding a person with a quiet demeanor, one who will work with little input from you?

- Do you cut things a little close, and want someone who will "look the other way"?

    Along with knowing what you are generally looking for, you will need to determine what things you cannot ever accept, such as:

- A person with a criminal record?

- A slap-on-the-back friendly, raucous person?

- A person with questionable ethics, (who might cheat)?

- A person with poor personal hygiene?

- A person with no training or experience?

- A person with a work history which shows that they stay in each job for only 6 months?

    The hiring goals that you develop will be for a combination of experience and attitudes that you are willing to work with.

CHAPTER 3...HIRING: WHAT ARE THE RULES OF THIS GAME?

A Story About the Irate Employee

Allen was an employee who was generally displeased with anything that his supervisor asked him to do. He complained a lot, and recently had begun to refuse to do certain tasks. Allen was an hourly employee with no paid vacation or medical benefits. After much thought, Allen's supervisor decided what he would do the next time Allen refused to do a task. He did not have to wait long to try his new idea. Allen reported to work on Monday morning, his supervisor asked him to unload a truck and take it to be washed, and Allen refused:

"That is Jim's job. Wait until Jim is free. I won't do Jim's work for him."

Allen's supervisor replied:

"That is the work that I have for you to do today. Since you won't do it, you can go home. Come back tomorrow if you are ready to do work. Also, you will be working a total of 8 fewer hours this week, since you refused to work today."

Allen was surprised at this turn of events, but had a response which he had used on past supervisors:

"When I was hired, I was told that I would only have to do this one job. It is illegal to assign me different jobs and it is illegal to give me fewer than 40 hours of work in a week. Also, it is illegal to not have medical leave and vacation days. I'll go home, but I'm calling my attorney about this."

Allen's supervisor was a little shaken by this outburst, but he kept his composure and returned to his office. He searched his memory and just was not sure what his legal requirements were. It did not seem logical to him that he be required to provide 40 hours of work for an employee who refused to do work, but he was not sure. He was also not certain what Allen was promised when he was hired. Could it be that Allen was promised that he would do only one type of work? He wondered if he should call his lawyer. He worried about that also, it might cost too much to get his lawyer's opinion. Finally he decided that if it was "illegal" then there must be a law written down somewhere. He decided to call his lawyer and ask about that.

Analysis: You Will Need to Learn About Employment Law

If you are going to hire and employ someone, it is best if you are aware of the laws governing your actions. Oftentimes, new supervisors become very confused over employment laws. Much of the confusion stems from the fact that what is legal and illegal is mostly discussed by people who really do not know.

If there is a law about something, then it is written down. If you are wondering if a law applies to what you are doing, then you should find it and read it. You will either find these laws in your local library or in a law library. A law library can often be found associated with a county courthouse or a law school. In a law library you will be able to find the books carrying the actual laws. In addition, you will find helpful services which produce books with both the law and explanations of it. These services also give references to court cases which have been tried over the various aspects of a particular law. You do not need to be a lawyer to read the law. It is a little slow at first, but with the help of a law dictionary you should have no problem. Your librarian will be able to point you in the right direction.

There is just no option but to read the law yourself. Talking to someone does not work. Everyone puts their own interpretation on the law, even your lawyer. Read it yourself, and decide for yourself.

Most of the confusion regarding employment law comes from the fact that there are actually different systems under which people are hired. Some people are "at will employees", some people are hired under the terms and conditions of union contracts, and some people have specific employment contracts

Types of Employment...Employment at Will

The great majority of us are "employees at will". Black's Law Dictionary defines this as:

"Either employer or employee may terminate their relationship at any time for any reason....without cause."

This is easiest to understand when comparing it to month to month renting of an apartment. Either the tenant or the landlord may terminate their agreement at any time.

The laws governing "at will" employment are those made by the state which you live in and the federal government. These laws address, but are not limited to, such items as the "minimum wage" and "family leave". These are the laws which you will need to read regarding your employee.

Types of Employment...Unions

Unions and management create contracts which define the conditions of employment.   If you are an employer of union personnel, you should sit down with the contract that your company and your union created and read it. If there are parts of it which you do not understand, go to the library and consult a law dictionary. The real point is, this document defines the rules which you must adhere to when dealing with your employees.   When you understand it, you will understand what your restrictions are and what restrictions your employee has. The union contract cannot supersede the local, state, and federal laws, but it can add more conditions and restrictions.

Types of Employment...Contracts

Some employees are hired with contracts.   Most often one hears of contracts relating to senior personnel at large corporations, TV and movie personalities, and public school district administration.   Employment contracts often have unusual and stringent restrictions for the employee.   They may require the employee to live in a particular area, to work a certain number of years, and in some cases, may even restrict the work that the employee is allowed to do after termination of the employment. If you are about to hire someone with a contract, you need to read the contract over carefully, first. This contract, as long as it is within local, state, and federal law, will govern your relationship with your employee.

CHAPTER 4...HIRING: ADVERTISING THE POSITION

A Story About the Particular Homemaker

Ruth and Bob made their company into one which was "home-life friendly". They had several newer features that many of their staff enjoyed. They had a flexible work schedule; "Get the job done, we don't care when you do it", they would often say. Many of their staff members worked out of home offices. Some staff members had regular non-work commitments which occurred during "traditional" work hours.

Ruth and Bob had a position open and wanted to make sure that the applicants would know about their nice work life. Their ad said, "Part time in your home, part time in our office". They received many telephone calls, all of which came with odd inquiries and comments:

"How far is it to your office from my house?"

"I'm willing to come in only once a week, if more than that is required, I won't take the job."

"How many hours would I be paid for?"

"What exactly is the job? If it involves a computer I won't take it."

During the interviews, they were told many surprising things, which were generally presented as conditions that Ruth and Bob would have to meet if they were lucky enough to have this person decide to work for them:

"My husband gets sick often, I would be unavailable for up to a week at a time."

"I would only be available to work after 10 AM."

"I would need to be paid for mileage when I came to the office."

"I would not be able to work after 5 PM, ever."

Ruth and Bob talked to more than ten people during that interviewing week and found no acceptable candidates.

Analysis: Advertise the Job, Not the Benefits

Ruth and Bob's problem was that they advertised the nice benefits of the job, rather than the actual requirements of the job. People who really did not want to work, but did want to earn money while relaxing at home, poured out of the woodwork. They determined that since Ruth and Bob seemed so nice and giving with their work conditions, more conditions could be added with no problem. Ruth and Bob never advertised the work at home feature of the job again. They barely mentioned it in the interview either.

Make Your Ad Tell About Your Hiring Goals

Your advertisement needs to attract the people who you want to hire. Ruth and Bob's ad attracted many people but no one who they were interested in. Your advertisement needs to tell as much as possible about the type of person which you want to hire. If there is an education requirement, it must be in the ad. If there is an ethic, or attitude requirement, it must be in the ad.

A Story About A Better Ad

Bob wrote a better ad, as follows:

COORDINATOR
To locate, hire, and expedite supply services for use in hazardous waste remediation business.

Must have:
- Intelligence
- Extreme flexibility
- "Whatever it takes" attitude
- Courage
- Tact
- Purchasing skills

Schedule of work is unpredictable, but need is generally dire.

To inquire call:

The number of sincerely interested people remained about the same, however the number of people who had "conditions of employment" to impose went to zero.

Summary

Make sure when you advertise for a job that you clearly tell who you are looking for. You are looking for a person who wants to do the work which you have to offer. You do not want a person who is only interested in the side benefits of the position.

CHAPTER 5...HIRING: READING THE RESUME

Now that you have at least thought through your hiring goals and determined how you will advertise the job, it is time to read over the resumes which have come your way.

A Story About an Easy Decision

Kathryn had been reviewing resumes for many years. She often tried to concentrate and read every word of the introductory letter, and the resume, but she generally could not. She found that she would skim it over and get a feeling about the person. She was in her office working quietly, when the door opened and a stranger walked in. The stranger, it turned out, was a person who had telephoned the week before to ask about jobs. They had decided to "drop by" and drop off their resume. Kathryn was faced with trying to be polite, while showing the person the door. She decided to keep the person standing, and to look briefly over the resume. What she found made it difficult for her to keep a straight face. The person had a brief cover letter, followed by a one page resume and that was followed by many certificates and letters of recommendation. But that was not what made her chuckle. What was so funny was that one of the letters was to a judge, written in the applicant's behalf, requesting leniency in the decision which was to be made.

Kathryn quickly explained again that there were no positions open, but that she would keep the resume information on file.

Analysis: You are Looking for 100% Failure Points

No one can read a resume and determine if the candidate will succeed in their company. However, with experience, anyone can look at a resume and determine the factors which tell them that they are 100% sure that the candidate will NOT succeed.   When you find a candidate who will not succeed, you do not need to waste your time with an interview.

The ability to make "100% will not succeed" decisions is gained primarily through personal experience after interviewing many people.

In the last story, Kathryn knew right away that she did not want to deal with an employee who had been in trouble with the law and who felt that a good reference was one which his previous employer had written to the judge on his behalf. She had had employees with "spotty" legal backgrounds, but none who bragged about it.

Use the resume reading to screen out those people who you know from previous experience have no chance of succeeding in your organization. Interview the rest.

A Story About a Delivery

A prospective employee called Ronald's office. They asked about jobs and Ronald suggested that they send a resume. They asked to whom they should send the resume and Ronald carefully spelled his last name, Smythe. The person repeated it. Then Ronald gave the office address. 3897 State Road 3, Jonesville, Ohio. He said to send the information to him and he would look it over. A few days later an envelope arrived in the mail. The address looked like this:

Mrs. Ronald Smyt

Personal Department

397 Circle Route 3

Jonesville, OH

Analysis: The Way In Which the Resume is Delivered Tells You Something About the Person

The first bit of data which a prospective employee will give you comes with the delivery of their information.

Ask yourself, did it come in the mail? If it did, is it addressed correctly? Did it come over the fax machine? If it did, is the cover page clear? Does it look like this is a gung-ho person who has their own personal fax machine, or are they "borrowing" their employer's machine?

Did the person personally deliver the resume? If they did, was it after you told them to mail it? Were they respectful of your need to keep the initial meeting brief, or did they attempt to force you into doing a spontaneous interview?

A Story About Stationery

James was looking for potential candidates for an open engineering position. He had a stack of resumes to look through. One caught his attention. It was on blue paper, with blue printing. In the upper right hand corner, there was a picture of a tennis racket. James thought it was odd, why would an engineer choose to have a tennis racket on his stationery?

Analysis: You Can See How Much the Person Wants the Job

Look over the paper that the resume is on. Does it look like the person thought a lot about it? Were they paying a lot of money in order to impress you? Are you impressed?

Do not discount handwritten resumes on notebook paper. Are they neat? Did the person put some work into it?

Is the cover letter well written? Is it long and boring? Is it short and concise? Does it actually say anything, or is it just polite ramblings? Is it even included?

Is the resume well written? Is it brief? Does it tell you about the person's education and training? Does it show you a consistent employment history? Is it written by hand? Are words spelled correctly?

In the story, James determined that a person who had stationery with a tennis racket on it was not too serious about being an engineer.

A Story About Attachments

Suzie had spent a week interviewing potential candidates for a supervisory position. She went to the outer office to meet the next applicant. The applicant, whose name was Peg, was passably dressed and was carrying a large notebook. Suzie escorted Peg into her office. She began to ask questions and in response to each question, Peg opened the notebook and showed Suzie a letter of recommendation or certificate which detailed the work that she had done. Suzie was impressed with Peg's organization. Suzie even felt a little bad that in her years of work, she had not ever gotten so many letters and certificates. Suzie hired Peg.

Over the next several weeks, Suzie was at times concerned, and at times alarmed by her new employee. Peg seemed to be working very hard, but not much was being accomplished. Peg seemed to not actually understand the work which she said she was capable of doing in the interview. Peg also made some company operating policy changes without asking any questions or getting permission. Suzie felt like she was chasing Peg around making sure that she would not get out of control.

Suzie began to think about the letters of recommendation which Peg had brought and also about the circumstances around Peg's recent "layoff" from her previous job. Suzie became fairly certain that Peg could not perform the job that she was hired for. She spoke with Peg, and Peg accepted Suzie's thoughts without argument.

Analysis: Attachments Are Not Necessarily a Good Thing

When looking over the resume, notice if there are attachments. If there are, how many? Do they relate to the job at hand? Generally, people who have lots of letters of recommendation, are people who have solicited them. If a supervisor is asked to provide a letter, they will most often provide one which is diplomatic.

If the attachments are in the form of certificates, consider that everyone accumulates these, most people lose them. Few people keep them for future interviews.

Summary

You should carefully consider the written information which a prospective employee gives you, and the manner in which it is delivered. Using the data which you accumulate, you will be able to identify people who you know with 100% certainty will <u>not</u> succeed in your company. Send those people a polite note. The rest of the people you should interview.

CHAPTER 6...HIRING: INTERVIEW QUESTIONS

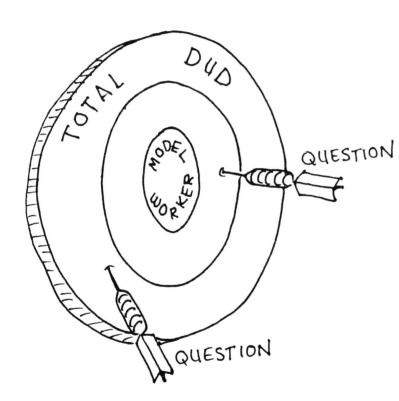

A Story About an Interview in 1975

Ruth was about to graduate from college. She started to work on her resume. She went to the Career Planning and Placement Office and got an instruction sheet showing how to make up a resume. She sat down at her electric typewriter and started to work.

At the top of the resume she included the generally accepted data: her name, her race, her weight, her health status, her marital status and the fact that she had no children. Next she included her education and past work experience. Last she listed references.

Ruth went to an interview for a job which she wanted very much. She was very nervous. Two people sat down to interview her. They told her that since she already worked for them in another capacity, they really did not need to ask her about her knowledge of the job.   But they did need some important information. They said:

"We know that you are going to get married in a few weeks, but we don't know if you are going to use the birth control pill?"

Ruth was a bit surprised, but she really wanted the job, so she replied truthfully, "

"Yes, I will be using the birth control pill."

That was not quite enough information for the interviewers:

"Are you planning to have children in the next five years?"

Ruth again, truthfully replied:

"We are in fact planning to work for the next five years, and then decide about starting a family."

Ruth did get the job. After she had been working for a few months, her supervisor told her all about the questions that employers really should not ask at an interview. Interestingly enough, her supervisor included in her list, most of the questions that had been asked of Ruth in her interview. The supervisor explained that even though those questions should not be asked, they had still needed the information. They claimed to need the information, in order to ensure that Ruth would stay working for them for at least the next three years. They did not want to go to the effort of training her, if she was planning to move on.

Analysis: Some Questions Have No Place In An Interview

When you are interviewing someone you want to know what they can do in relation to the skills which you need, and you want to know what sorts of attitudes they have toward working. Questions of a personal nature have no bearing on either of these areas. You cannot assume, for instance, if a woman or a man plan to have a child in the near future, that they will necessarily quit their job. You cannot even assume that they will do a job of a lesser quality. The thing which will determine the quality of job that they do is their overall work ethic and attitude. In Ruth's case, she actually stayed at the job for four years, while the two people interviewing her left after two years.

You might want to ensure that a new employee will stay working for you for a certain number or years, or will remain single or childless, but, unless you are going to have an employment contract drawn up and make these things conditions of the job, you cannot discuss them in the interview. You have to choose your new employee based on what skills and personality they have, and then you can try to create a work environment such that they will stay working for you for a long time to come.

These are several things which you should not ask about in an interview for an "at will employee" because they have no relevance to the quality of work that the person will do, and thus no relevance to the job:

- A person's sexual activities outside of the work environment.

- A person's religion.

- A person's marital status.

- Details about a handicap which does not have any bearing on the job.

- A person's plans for having a family.

- How the person plans to deal with child care obligations.

One of the reasons that people want to ask these personal questions is that they are worried that the interviewee may not be able to handle the requirements of the job because of personal problems. If this is your concern, instead of asking personal questions, you simply need to clearly describe the parameters of the job and let the interviewee decide if they can do the job. You might say, "You may be called in to work during the dinner hour", "It is very important that our employees arrive punctually", or "Everyone is required to work one Sunday each month." If they decide that they can comply with the job requirements, then make your decision based on their ability to do the job.

Analysis: Interview Questions Should Be About Training and Work Ethics

Interview questions that you should ask are those dealing with the person's training and skills which are needed in the job, along with questions dealing with the person's work ethic.

TRAINING AND RELATED SKILLS:

These are the easy questions. You ask, generally while reading their resume, probing questions about their training:

- "What sorts of things did you study in college, related to your degree?"

- "What part did you take in the production of your company's annual report?"

- "How many Geology classes did you have?"

- "How many people were science majors at your college?"

- "Which computer programs are you familiar with?"

- "You say that you know how to program computers, what languages are you familiar with?"

- "You say that you can repair most vehicles, what about a 1947 Oliver tractor?"

WORK ETHIC:

- "Can you tell me about your most favorite and least favorite supervisor?"

- "What was your favorite job, and why?"

- "Have you ever been told by a supervisor not to do something, and then done it anyway?"

- "Have you ever quit a job, on the spot, on principle?"

- "Have you ever been fired from a job?"

- "Do you think that you were a good worker in your last job?"

- "Is there anything that you could have done better?"

Summary

Design your interview questions to help you determine if this is a person who you might want to have work for you. If there are special conditions with the job, make sure that you clearly explain them and then allow the interviewee to determine if they will be able to handle them. Do not judge the interviewee's personal life, only their skills and capabilities.

CHAPTER 7...HIRING: THE INTERVIEW

Most people think that the interview process will enable them to find the "perfect employee". They believe that during the interview which lasts from as little as one hour to as long as one day, they will be able to ask enough question and make enough observations to determine if the person is the one who they are looking for.

When this idea is compared to other relationships, such as dating and marriage, it becomes obvious that it would be nearly impossible to make this decision in the amount of time which is allowed. The interview has to be a continuation of the search for any of the known 100% failure traits. If the applicant has any of the traits which you know 100% of the time will cause them to fail as an employee, you will not hire them. If not, and if they meet your goals in experience, background, and attitude, then you will consider hiring them.

A reminder: the 100% failure traits in no way relate to a person's sex, race, religion, or handicaps, only to their attitude, training, and experience.

A Story About Ted's First Interview

Ted was ready to do his first interview. The interviewee came on time, but Ted was involved with an employee, so he continued to talk with the employee and allowed the interviewee to wait. When he was ready, Ted introduced himself to the interviewee and took him to a corner of the office. Right after the interview started, Ted received a telephone call, which he took.

Then an employee came in with a question. When Ted had taken care of these interruptions he said to the person:

"The job that you will be doing will be in the file room. Everyone starts there and is promoted out in about six months."

Ted then asked the interviewee a series of questions and, after a few more interruptions, Ted concluded the interview.

Ted really did not like this candidate very well and was fairly certain that he would not hire him. He ushered the person out of the office with a final statement:

"Well, you seem like a promising candidate, I'll call you later in the week and tell you my decision."

Analysis: Don't Make it Sound Like the Candidate Already Has the Job

Ted was a regal supervisor. He was too concerned with making himself appear busy and important. By allowing himself to be interrupted, Ted was actually rude to the interviewee. Ted also made the same mistake that all first-time interviewers do, which is to phrase their information in a way that makes it sounds like the person already has the job. This generally happens because the interviewer is nervous, and does not want to make the interviewee feel bad. In Ted's case, he not only made it sound like the person would be working in the file room, he also offered them a promotion within six months! A better way to start the introduction to the job would be to say:

"Let me explain about the job for which you are interviewing today."

It is best to not be definite about raises and promotions in the interview. Candidates have a way of taking these bits of data as promises, and expecting them.

A Story About Some Past Work Experiences

Ann arrived for her interview on time. She was nicely and conservatively dressed. She seemed to be friendly. Her newly completed degree was exactly what the job needed. She spoke about her schooling. She also volunteered that she was wanting to leave her present job because the ladies in the office were "catty". Ann said:

"They are telling the supervisor that I am not carrying my fair share of the work load. It is simply not true, I work very hard."

Ann's interviewers liked her, and sympathized with her plight. After all, everyone has experienced "catty" co-workers. Ann was hired.

In the weeks to follow, Ann continued to be very friendly. She seemed organized and very neat. Any notes taken by Ann were legible and complete. Then, an office worker noticed that when Ann took a phone message, it took her a full fifteen minutes to fill out the message slip. She re-wrote it a few times, and seemed to write slowly. Two phone calls could consume over half an hour of Ann's time. Other workers noticed that when five o'clock came, Ann packed up and left, even if everyone else was planning to work until the task was completed.

Ann seemed to make the same mistakes which all new employee made, but after six months, she was still making those mistakes. When asked about it she replied:

"It's still all new to me."

It slowly became apparent to her supervisors that Ann's description of the "catty" people in her past office was really a warning flag. Ann's work performance was exactly as they said, she was slow and did not carry her share of the load.

Analysis: Listen to The Stories That Interviewees Tell You About Their Work Experiences

You want to ask questions which will cause the interviewee to tell you about their past work experiences. Then listen carefully to their answers. Think about your past experiences, do they match, or does this one sound odd? If Ann's supervisors had thought hard they would have remembered that any time that they were in an office and many of the workers complained that someone was not working hard enough, it was because the person was not working hard enough.

A Story About a Reference Check

Ann's employers figured that they had learned a valuable lesson. They began to ask all interviewees about their experience with co-workers. Aaron came for an interview. In response to the questions, he said that at his current job, the people accused him of not working hard enough. Ann's employer's knew that this was a warning flag for them. But, they did not want to be too harsh, and Aaron seemed like a very nice person. They decided that they would check out his story. They called the employer listed on Aaron's resume.

The previous employer told them that there were "catty complaints" about Aaron's work, but this was justified (perhaps inappropriately) as "ladies" complaints. His previous employer said that some people said that Aaron took too long to do his work, but that he thought Aaron was a "thinker". He also mentioned that Aaron would speak his mind.

Ann's employers decided that Aaron really seemed like a nice person, and they needed someone quickly. His previous supervisor said nothing bad about him, and some offices really are full of nasty people. Aaron was hired.

After about six months the employers discovered that Aaron took about three times as long to do a project as others, and that there were "catty complaints" but in this case males were making them.

Upon reviewing the notes which they took after Aaron's interview, the supervisors discovered that Aaron's previous supervisor had in fact politely described the very problem that they now had with Aaron.

Analysis: References Checks Are Not Worth a Lot

The problem with checking references, is that people giving references are never totally forthright. Previous employers do not often say bad things about their departed employees. They may be worried that the employee will hear what they said and get mad at them, or they may just know that it is not proper to say bad things about people.   Sometimes, they want to unload a bad employee, and so they actually give a good reference.

A Story About Money

Loren had a good degree in an up-and-coming field. The field was remotely related to the work that the company actually did. Loren was a smart person. He asked about money in his interview and let the employers know how much he expected to see.   With his impressive credentials, he was hired.   He immediately began to observe that he should be paid more because of his degree. Even though the company did not have any real need for his degree, they felt that in order to be competitive, they should give Loren more money. Along with it, they asked that he begin to develop contacts to bring in more work in his area. Loren continued to work hard, but he did not work on bringing in any new contracts.   Loren heard of someone in a position similar to his who was being paid one dollar an hour more than he was currently earning. Ignoring the fact that many others similarly employed earned less than he did, Loren went to his employers and told them that he would need more money. Once again his employers wanted to be competitive, and they wanted to keep Loren happy. They repeated that he needed to help get in work and gave him the raise.

Each week Loren sat down with one of his supervisors and discussed his future. Where was he going? What work was out there? How much money would he make in the end? He became an employee who needed more time than the others, and needed more money than the others. His supervisors kept hoping that it would all pay off in the product which he would produce.

Several months later Loren resigned. He said that the supervisors were not looking out for his interests and that the company did not do work in his exact field.

Analysis: Too Much Concern About Money Is Not Good

The least ideal interviewee asks first about money and benefits and second about the actual job. If you hire a person like this, they will be concerned about their money, their future, and their benefits during all of their tenure with you.

A Story About a Good Interview

Clara had been interviewing people for years. She had a private office which she used for these interviews. She had been to a people management course at Disney World and had learned that she had to decorate her office to show visitors what the company was like. This would allow the applicant to determine if this company was a place where they would like to work. She had tasteful pictures showing her company's products, and where applicable, she was using the actual products.

Clara knew that applicants often arrived early, so she was ready early herself. As soon as she saw a confused person entering the outer office she walked up to them:

"You must be Henry Jones, here for an interview"

She escorted Henry into the office and began:

"First let me tell you a little about the job which you are interviewing for."

She proceeded to explain to Henry about the actual job. Then she asked Henry about his background and experience. Finally she discussed a little bit about the company's history and ethics, work conditions, and benefits. She concluded:

"If you have no more questions, I want to thank you for coming today. I will be looking over a number of applicants, and will contact you one way or the other within two weeks."

Analysis: The Interviewee Is a Guest

All rules of etiquette apply during an interview. Treat your interviewees as you would a guest:

- Be ready when they arrive.

- Try to put them "at their ease".

- Give a clear introduction to the job which they are interviewing for.

- Tell them about the company.

- Be clear to them about when they will hear from you.

An interview process involves both you examining the potential candidates, and them examining you. Ask them questions about themselves. Allow them to ask questions about your company. You are going to determine if you want to hire them. Give them a chance to decide if they want to be hired by you.

A Story About a Hiring Decision

A potential candidate was interviewed by three supervisors on the staff. The supervisors met to discuss their "findings". Claire, who was a sensitive supervisor, recommended that they hire the person. She said:

"He seemed to be qualified, he was interested in us and he seemed to need the job."

Bradley, a belligerent supervisor, scoffed:

"Maybe he needed the job, but he asked about benefits, since he asked, we can't hire him."

Larry, a regal supervisor, looked worried and said:

"I didn't like how he answered the question about his least favorite supervisor. He said that the supervisor was like a dictator, and that means that he won't respect authority."

Analysis: It is Hard to Make the Decision to Hire Someone

Ultimately, you will have to make a decision to hire, or not to hire a particular person. Your goal is to get a good worker who fits the list of attributes which you originally set out to find.

The sensitive supervisor has a very big problem making the final decision. Even if they know that all of the signals are wrong, they do not want to hurt the applicant's feelings by not hiring them. Worse yet, the sensitive supervisor really does not want to make the telephone call to tell the person that they did not get the job.

It is helpful if the sensitive supervisor has another person to talk to. The sensitive supervisor can then tell the other person all that they are thinking about the applicants and the partner can summarize their decision. "It sounds like you liked Ed and are unsure about Jerry".

Postcards or letters can be sent to the people who are not chosen for the job, rather than calling them. This will ease the tension of the sensitive supervisor.

The belligerent supervisor is generally irritated that they have to take the time to do an interview. They want to be able to make a decision quickly. They want to either hire everyone, or hire no one. If they decide to hire everyone, they plan to "see how things work out". If they decide to hire no one, they make a list of "100% failure points" which is very long. Then, if the interviewee so much as sneezes, the belligerent supervisor, in this mode of thinking, rejects them.

The belligerent supervisor has to take the time to sit down and listen to the interviewee and really consider what they are told.

The regal supervisor tends to look at all job applicants as potential threats to their position. They generally find something to fault in everyone who they see. Creating an objective rating sheet which can be filled out after the interview might be useful to them.

Think Hard About Hiring Guidelines:

Each employer needs to make up their own personal list of "do not hire" traits, here is a basic list which you may want to choose from:

Think long hard before hiring a person if:

- They come very late for the interview or don't come at all, and have no valid reason, like "I broke my leg getting into my car".

- If they come for the interview in attire which you find to be inappropriate.

- If they come to the interview in dirty clothing without a valid reason like, "I got a flat tire, but wanted to be on time".

- If they are belligerent in the interview "Is that all the benefits that you are offering?" "When will I get vacation?".

- If they put conditions of employment upon you "I will have to have Wednesdays off".

- If they have a wild story about their past supervisor and the unfairness at the past office. These things do happen, but most of us don't talk about them in an interview.

- If they bring large files full of letters of recommendations. No one gets large files full of letters of recommendations unless they ask for them.

- If you are in fear of the person.

- If you instantly dislike the person.

- If you had an urge to pitch their resume in the wastebasket when you first received it.

Summary

You will not be able to find the perfect person. After you have looked over all of the potential candidates, and have removed those with traits which you know fail 100% of the time, you will be able to offer a job to those who are left. Sometimes, there is no one left. It is often better to go with a lower number of staff members, than to have problem employees.

CHAPTER 8...HIRING: THE JOB OFFER

Your first "supervisory experience" with your new employee will be when you offer them the job. While mistaken impressions can always be rectified, it is easier to start correctly. You are the supervisor and they are the employee. You would like them to work for you, and you feel that they are qualified, but you are not planning to beg them to take the job, nor are you planning to demean them.

A Story About a Good Job Offer

Clara had interviewed four potential candidates for the position which she had open. Two of the candidates said things during the interview which Clara knew would certainly cause them to fail in her organization. Of the remaining two, she felt that one was more qualified. She called Bartholomew back to offer him the position:

"I would like to offer you a job with our company. The starting wage is $7 per hour. If you would like the job, you could begin to work anytime within the next month. Do you have any questions about the offer, or the job? I am sure that you may want to think this over. Please call me back with your decision, do you have my phone number?"

A Story About a Bad Job Offer

Sam had interviewed 20 candidates for the open position. He had carefully selected the candidate which he wanted and he telephoned them to offer the job:

"I decided to offer you the job. There were several other people, and I really liked the guy who had been a salesman, but he had no training as an engineer, so you are left. The starting wage is $12 per hour, do you want it?"

Analysis of a Good Job Offer

A good job offer follows the lines of polite etiquette. You offer the job, and give them the opportunity to ask questions. You should always give them all of the data which they need in order to make their decision, but nothing else. Then, you allow them time to make their decision. Never presume that they will immediately accept the job.

Analysis of a Bad Job Offer

A bad job offer is one where you look weak and undecided. It is also one which makes the person feel either one extreme of "second best" or the other extreme of "the candidate you cannot live without". If you begin either of these two ways, you will have newly created potential supervisory problems. These supervisory problems can be overcome, but it is much better to start the work relationship with mutual respect rather than hurt feelings or inflated egos.

The Three Supervisors and Job Offers

The sensitive supervisor wants to make sure that the person will not have hurt feelings. They tend to want to offer more money, and tell the person things like "you are the best candidate we have ever seen". Since they have only known the person for about an hour, this is often overstated, and may cause the person to swagger into their new job, feeling that they are better than all of the current employees.

The belligerent supervisor often thinks of the job offer as a test of the new employee. They want to offer the candidate a slightly lower salary in order to see if they will take the job anyway. They want to test to see if the new employee is "tough enough".

The regal supervisor is still worried that this person may take their job. They tend to fashion the offer so that the person feels put down by saying things like: "There were better people than you, but they turned us down, you are actually our third choice".

All three supervisor personalities need to concentrate on being professional and polite.

A Word About Job Negotiations

Once the offer is on the table, the job candidate may want to enter into negotiations for wages, work schedule or benefits. We all know that the purchase of an automobile or a house involves negotiation. The negotiations for work conditions have no set rules. Some companies negotiate and some do not. This is a situation where the candidate has a problem. Are they expected to negotiate or not? If they do not, will they potentially lose out on money? If they do, will they offend the company? To ease the situation, the thoughtful supervisor might mention during the offer whether negotiating is done at their company or not. In this way, both parties will be "playing the same game".

CHAPTER 9...HIRING: THE ORIENTATION

A Story About Bob's First Day Of Work

Bob had his Master's Degree firmly in hand. He had interviewed with several large oil companies, and one utility company. He decided that his career would be better served by the utility company. Bob was a small town boy, having spent most of his formative years in a city of less than 4,000 people. He did not like large cities, but nonetheless accepted the job in New York City. He and Ruth packed up and made the journey to the "big city". The movers who arrived cautioned them about all of the evils of the city.

They were set up in their hotel, awaiting the availability of their apartment and Bob took his first mass transit commute to work. He walked up to the office building, which easily housed as many people as his entire home town. He found his way to the office where he had had his interview 4 months earlier and found his new supervisor.

His new supervisor looked up from his desk and asked:

"Who are you?"

Bob replied:

"I'm Bob Haag, your new engineer."

After some discussion, the new supervisor did vaguely remember that he had hired Bob.

Analysis: Remember Who You Hired

The first and most obvious part of new employee orientation is to remember who you hired. Bob certainly was very worried when it looked like he might not have a job. Along with this, it is important to remember what day the new person is to arrive, and to be prepared to receive them.

A Story About a New Employee at Haag Environmental Company

Maude was just hired as a beginning scientist at Haag Environmental Company. She was asked to come in to the office on Friday afternoon to fill out her paperwork. Her supervisor met with her and explained her hire letter, her tax forms, and about the physical which she would need to take in the next week. In addition, Maude was given her uniforms and a brief list of things which she would need to take care of in the next week. She was asked to return at 8:00 AM Monday morning when the entire staff would be present for their monthly training.

Maude was nervous, but arrived on Monday morning, wearing her new uniform. She was relieved when she spotted her supervisor near the door as she arrived. Her supervisor showed her into the meeting room, offered her some food and suggested a place for her to sit. As staff members arrived, Maude was introduced. She then listened to the hour of training which followed.

As soon as the meeting was over, Maude was told that she would be meeting with the lead technical person to learn about what the company did and how it did it. Her supervisor took her and introduced her to the technical manager.

After that meeting, Maude needed a rest and was given her Health and Safety Manual to read. Throughout the week Maude was taken to meet the department heads of all of the areas. Each time, her supervisor took her and introduced her. Each meeting lasted less than one hour.

At one point in the week Maude was told it was time for her History class. She was really wondering about it, until she discovered that it was a lecture about the history of the company. She found that she was gaining a sense of how the company did things and why they did what they did.

In between her meetings, her supervisor started her working on her actual job. Each part of the job was given to her in pieces and carefully explained.

During the second week, Maude was with her supervisor less and less and was able to perform her new duties better. She felt comfortable asking for help when she needed it and was beginning to feel like a member of the staff.

Analysis: The Goal of Orientation-Make Them Become a Part Of Your Organization

Your orientation program needs to be designed so that the new employee discovers as quickly as possible how things are done in your company, and what their role is to be. Ideally, the supervisor of the employee will perform most of the orientation functions.

CHAPTER 10...FIRING: PERFORMANCE PROBLEMS WHICH ARE NOT REAL

A Story About an Anxious Owner

Hubert owned his own business. He published books. He was lucky enough to have had a tremendously successful first five years of business. He had discovered several very talented authors and they had become overnight successes. Now, heading into year 6, Hubert could see that his business was not doing as well as in past years. Hubert decided that his vice-president for sales and marketing was probably the cause. She must be slacking off. Hubert fired Edith and hired a recent graduate from Harvard. After six months Hubert saw no improvement in sales so he fired and hired again. Hubert kept this system up for three years, and his business continued to make a profit, but it never did as well as it had those first five years. Hubert determined that vice-presidents just weren't what they used to be.

Analysis: Not All Business Problems Are Caused By Employees

Hubert obviously had a problem differentiating between cycles in business and employee performance problems. He figured that a "knight in shining armor" would ride in and make him the profits that he had once seen. It is obviously very important to be able to determine if your problems are due to the general market, or due to an employee. Hubert probably fired a very capable person when he fired Edith. He never had a chance to see if his next vice-presidents were any good, because he only gave them each 6 months to perform. Perhaps if he had given each of them a few years to work at their positions he might have seen a difference in his bottom line.

A Story About a Long Term Worker

Ruth started work at a museum as a full-time employee three weeks after she graduated from college. She had worked as a part-time time employee for the two previous years and felt that she knew most of what it took to do the job. In the first few months, on several occasions, she took telephone calls from teachers who were upset about something having to do with their scheduled field trip. Ruth really did not know what to say to the teachers and had to refer the calls to her supervisor. Her supervisor explained to her that it would take Ruth an entire year to really learn all that there was to know about the business they were in. At the end of the year, Ruth agreed. How could something as simple as working in a museum be that complicated?

A few years later, Ruth found herself facing a group of 60 third graders who had come to the museum without a reservation. The museum was full of reserved groups and had no room to hold them right then. It took 30 very long minutes, talking with angry teachers, before Ruth figured out how to solve this problem.

A few years later still, Ruth discovered that while she had scheduled 30 preschoolers for a visit, the teacher had brought 60. She had no problem. She called her staff and they greeted all of the preschoolers. The visit worked as if it had been planned with 60 students all along.

Analysis: It Takes Time to Learn to Do a Job Well

No matter how simple a job looks, it takes at least a year for an employee to learn all of the aspects of it. If the job involves operating a machine, the employee has to learn the particular foibles of that particular machine with all of the stresses which are put on it. If the job is dealing with the public, the employee has to go through all of the problems which could occur, with all of the types of people who deal with the employee's company.

The learning process for a particular employee can be sped up with some side-by-side training by an experienced "older" employee, but it will still take some time. That is why there is the adage "experience is the best teacher".

At times, supervisors determine that if the new employee does not know all of the aspects of the job within six months, it is time to call it quits and look for someone else. An experienced employee is invaluable. Do not confuse lack of experience with lack of ability.

CHAPTER 11...FIRING: PERFORMANCE PROBLEMS WHICH CAN BE FIXED

A Story About a Performance Problem

Ned noticed that his clerk Josh was not getting his work done. Ned thought about Josh's schedule and decided that nothing at work had changed. He decided to check it out on a low level, when he next saw Josh he asked:

"Josh, how are things going?"

Josh responded:

"O.K., I guess, I have a lot on my mind."

Ned briefly thought about this and then said:

"Is there anything going wrong at work that I can help with?"

Josh replied:

"No, it is my teenager, Clara, she is dating a boy who I don't like."

Ned then said:

"Josh, you may not know this, but it is affecting your work. You have not completed an assignment on time in over a week, and that is not normal performance for you."

Analysis: Some Performance Problems Can Be Fixed

Everyone has performance problems at some time or another. Those employees who really want to work and want to do a good job, are generally very receptive to a constructive talk from their supervisor.

It is helpful if the supervisor thinks about the problem a little before they meet with the employee. Has anything changed recently at work? Are there new employees? Are there new work assignments?

The supervisor needs to determine if this is a major problem that requires a formal meeting, or a more minor problem that can be solved with a brief and informal, but private meeting.

When talking with the employee, the supervisor needs to make sure that they give the employee a chance to talk. People who are having problems generally know that they are having problems, but would rather be able to tell you, than to have you tell them. If you do announce to them that they have a problem, they will be defensive and your talk will not go well. A good opening line is: "How are things going?" If a personal problem is brought up, the supervisor should not become involved in solving it, but rather tell the employee the facts about the performance which they have seen.

Other easy-to-fix performance problems may be caused by the work environment. The employee may not like a co-worker, or they may simply be bored.

A good employee will always respond to a frank talk about a performance problem. After a brief, constructive discussion with the employee, you should notice an improvement within 24 hours.

Sometimes however, after all of your careful work in the interviewing and hiring process, and your frank talk about performance problems, the employee does not respond. These are the employees who may need to be fired.

CHAPTER 12...FIRING: WHEN TO THINK ABOUT FIRING

A Story About a Bad Employee

Roxanne had hired Raymond as a favor to another department in the company. They did not have the budget to support Raymond, but told Roxanne that he was a good proposal estimator, and they did not want to see him without a job.

For the first few months, Raymond appeared to be a good worker. Then he began to complain about things. He told Roxanne that his desk was really not large enough for the work that he did. He explained that he would not be able to get the estimate done on time because he did not have enough space. Roxanne responded by getting a larger desk for Raymond. Then he told Roxanne that the proposal that he was working on was stupid, that the company could not ever get the job anyway, so he did not need to get his part of it done, and besides his cubicle was dark and dreary. Roxanne figured that maybe if Raymond were nearer to sunlight, he would be happier. She re-arranged the office so that Raymond was nearer to the windows. Raymond continued to complain.

Finally Roxanne called Raymond into her office and said to him:

"Raymond, you are always unhappy. It is affecting your work. I have made all of the physical changes to your office space that I can. Now it is time for you to improve your attitude."

Analysis: Some People Are Bad Employees

Sometimes, supervisors work so hard on creating an environment where their employee can succeed that they miss the fact that the employee is just not a good worker.

Raymond was shifted from another department, a sure sign that all was not perfect. When he was unhappy with his office, he simply did not do his work. Unhappy good workers still work. Problem employees stop working entirely.

Warning Signs Of Problem Employees

- You have given them several "Your performance is slacking off" talks and have seen no improvement.

- You are rearranging where they sit, in the hopes that they will work better.

- You are doing their work for them.

- They refuse to work until you do some action.

- They routinely defy company rules.

CHAPTER 13...FIRING: HOW TO FIRE

A Story About a Firing

Gertrude was an employee who had a pre-conceived disrespect for anyone whose job title was "supervisor". She was sure that all supervisors were in luxurious offices, drinking expensive flavored coffee, while she worked hard in the copy room. She found opportunities to tell other staff members about how terrible her supervisor, Shirley, was whenever they came into the copy room. She took small statements made by Shirley and used them to support her feelings.   When Shirley changed everyone's work schedule in order to accommodate a surprise audit, Gertrude was heard to say:

> "Can you believe that she changed my work schedule again? If she could just plan better she would be able to give me a regular schedule!"

After listening to Gertrude, other employees began to feel that Shirley was indeed unfair to Gertrude, and maybe to them also. Shirley began to notice that in her weekly meetings, Gertrude always had a sour look on her face, and often challenged Shirley's statements. Shirley decided to hold the meeting in a larger room and Gertrude said:

> "That is stupid to move us, we can all fit in, you just want to stand farther away from us!"

Shirley did her best to keep control of her staff at her meetings, but she could see that Gertrude's copy room talking was eroding Shirley's position and making the staff work inefficiently. Shirley became more and more angry. Finally, one day it was too much. Shirley called Gertrude on the copy room telephone and said:

> "Gertrude, you are insubordinate. I had hoped that you would stop your behavior, but you have not, so I have no choice but to fire you. Please gather up your things and leave within an hour."

Gertrude was surprised and irritated. She made sure that she stayed around the office for the next three hours, so that she could tell everyone how unreasonable Shirley was. After she left she applied for unemployment benefits. The unemployment office contacted Shirley and Shirley told them that Gertrude was fired for a just cause. The unemployment office asked Shirley to send them her documentation of the problem. Shirley had no documentation. Gertrude received her unemployment benefits. This made Shirley angrier still. Gertrude also considered filing a discrimination lawsuit against the company.

Analysis: Shirley Did a Few Things Wrong

You can fire a person for any reason that you want to, but if you do it with no justification, you may create yourself a legal nightmare. In fact, the ramifications of firing a person are often scary enough that some supervisors opt to just tolerate the behavior or to try to transfer the person to another department. The problem with either of these approaches is that a poor performer brings everyone down with them. Other employees do not like having to do the work of the lazy person. Other employees can be incited to rebel by a poor employee. Other people may be physically in danger if there is an employee who ignores safety rules. Even though it is hard to do, you must remove people who are not performing.

There are two "musts" when you are planning to fire a person:

- You must give them a clear explanation of the problem and a chance to improve.

- You must document everything.

Shirley allowed the situation with Gertrude to be controlled by her emotions. She was very irritated by Gertrude and finally fired her when she could not take it anymore. But she had never even confronted Gertrude.

Gertrude was never told that if she persisted in her behavior, she would be fired. She was given no chance to improve herself. She was justified in deciding that it was an unfair firing.

Who Cares If Benefits Are Given Or If There Is a Lawsuit?

Some supervisors have a bit of a cavalier attitude toward the potential after-effects of firing a person, they are often heard to say:

"Our insurance rates will go up, but at least the person is gone! If there is a lawsuit, it will be less costly than the damage the person was doing."

Their statements are accurate but hard to understand, why go to the expense of defending a lawsuit and paying higher unemployment premiums if you don't need to?

A Story About a Better Firing

Shirley and her staff settled down to work after Gertrude was gone. Shirley hired a new technician who seemed to be working out well. After six months, Shirley noticed that Albert, the technician, was taking some long breaks from work. In fact, he was coming in on time, and having some coffee, meeting all of the other staff members as they came in, and discussing what they were going to do that day. By about 10:00 AM, Albert would start to work, but he would be back in the coffee room at 11:30 AM and have a lunch break until 1:30 PM.

Albert became such a fixture that newer employees began to take work direction from him. Shirley could not believe her bad luck.

Shirley found Albert in the coffee room in the morning. She asked him to come to her office with her. After he had sat down she said:

"I am concerned about your work. When you started with us you were quite dedicated, but lately it seems like you spend more time on breaks than doing actual work. This is showing up in your projects, they are not getting done. Also, you have been giving direction to the new staff. That is my job."

Albert replied:

"Some things are going wrong around here. I am just trying to help, these people are confused."

Shirley said:

"Albert, the problem is that you are not getting your work done. Do you understand your task list? Is it too long or confusing?"

Albert said:

"Oh, I understand the task list and know that you want the work done. I do the work on my list that seems important to me, I let the other work slide. I really don't like to have to complete tasks with a deadline. I like to take breaks. The work will all get done eventually."

Shirley said firmly:

"Albert, you are not getting your work done. Also, you are giving directions to people who are not yours to supervise. You must start doing your work, and stop supervising staff members. We will meet again in two weeks. At that time, you need to have completed your task list. Either you will have improved, or you will be fired."

Albert appeared to consider these words and then said:

"I really need this job. I am getting the work done eventually. It almost seems unreasonable to expect me to finish my task list each week."

Shirley explained that each person on the staff was expected to finish their task list each week. Albert left the room with a bit of a confused look on his face.

Shirley carefully wrote notes of the meeting that she had with Albert. She dated the pages and signed them. Over the next two weeks she made sure that Albert had a clear written list of his tasks, and on her copy of the list she wrote when the task was assigned and when it was completed. She also documented Albert's arrival and departure times, along with the length of his breaks.

After one week, Shirley spoke briefly with Albert at his station:

"Albert, I have assigned you work this week, and it is nearly Friday, and none of the work is done. This is exactly what I was talking about last week. You have to get your work done."

Albert protested:

"You gave me too long of a list. I would have to work overtime to get it done!"

Shirley said firmly:

"The list was not too long. If you had started on it on Monday you would be done already. You had better get started working."

Shirley documented this meeting also.

At the end of the next week, Albert still had not improved and Shirley called him into her office one last time:

"Albert, we spoke two weeks ago, and again last week. You have had two weeks to improve your performance, and you have not done so. You did not get the tasks which I assigned you done. You are fired."

To this Albert replied:

"If I had known that you were serious, I would have worked harder. You are pretty unreasonable. There are a lot of things wrong with this organization, a lot of people are pretty upset and are ready to quit. Jim says that I do good work. You gave me a raise 6 weeks after I started. You have been acting like you have a personal vendetta against me for the past month. I may have to call my lawyer about this!"

Shirley escorted Albert to the door. As they got to the door, Albert turned and asked:

"Will you give me a recommendation for my next job?"

Shirley did not allow him to say goodbye to the other staff members. She immediately went and wrote down what was said during this last meeting. She did not have time to use her computer, as she had before. She found a nice piece of blank paper and wrote the notes by hand with a felt-tip pen. She initialed the notes and added them to Albert's file.

Next, Shirley called her staff together. She briefly told them:

"Unfortunately, I had to fire Albert today. He was not doing his job. I had warned him several times, but he refused to improve."

A week later, Shirley received a notice from the unemployment office. The rather confusing form seemed to tell her that Albert had filed for unemployment and that he would receive it. Shirley took the notice and immediately went to work. She wrote in the blank area:

"I am contesting this determination. Albert was informed that he was performing poorly, he was given a chance to improve, and he did not. He was warned and then he was fired."

Shirley filled out the space that stated that it would be best for the unemployment office to call her in the afternoon of any week day. Shirley took the option of faxing the form back to the unemployment office. She wanted to make sure that it got to them within the filing limit.

About a week later, in the morning, Shirley received a call from the unemployment office. The person asked her if Albert was qualified for the job which he had. Shirley replied:

"Yes, he had a two year degree in the field."

They asked if Albert had had difficulties with the job from the beginning. To this Shirley said:

"No, to begin with he did the job well."

They asked if Albert had a clear idea of what he was supposed to accomplish each day, and if he had been given a chance to improve. Shirley described to the person the steps which she had taken. They asked if there was any documentation. Shirley agreed to fax her file.

Analysis: Good Reasons to Fire a Person

It is reasonable to fire a person because:

- They are capable of doing their job, but they are not doing it, and you have warned them.

- They are disruptive to the staff, and you have asked them to stop.

- They do not come to work on time, and you have a company policy that says they must.

- They do not come to work at all, do not call, and you have a company policy that says they must.

- They endanger the lives of others on the staff and they have been told not to.

- They break the law while doing their job.

- They harass other employees, because of race, sex, or religion.

The overriding theme here, is that it is reasonable to fire a person if you have a company policy about an action and/or you have given documented instruction to the person regarding an action. The requirement must seem reasonable to most people. The employee must be given a chance to improve.

Bad Reasons to Fire a Person

It is not reasonable to fire a person because:

- You don't like the religion that they practice.

- You are jealous of them.

- They know too much for their job.

- You have recently moved them to a job that they are unqualified for and they cannot do it.

- You don't like their race.

- You don't like their suspected sexual activities outside of work.

- They have a long-term, expensive disease.

- Their family is pushing up the company medical insurance rates.

- You suspect that they have a substance abuse problem.

- You are tired of them.

More About Shirley

The day after Shirley fired Albert she was surprised to note that she felt very bad about the entire thing. She wondered to herself over and over if she had done the right thing, if she had warned Albert enough, and she also worried about the "problems with the staff" that Albert alluded to.

By the next week, Shirley noted that the staff did not appear to have any problems. In fact, many of them had made references to Albert, but in a way of relief that he was gone. They said things like:

"Now we have the coffee room back to ourselves, I am much happier without those conflicting directions".

Summary of How to Fire

- Make sure it is for a work related performance problem.

- Give warning.

- Give a clear concrete plan of what needs to be improved.

- Give enough time for the person to improve.

- Document everything.

- Give a "final warning".

- Fire the person in private.

- Escort them out of the building.

- Make sure that you tell the rest of the staff about it, afterwards, briefly, and all at the same time.

The Three Supervisors and Firing

The sensitive supervisor does not have any real trouble firing employees. This is because the sensitive supervisor has generally given the employee more help than they should have. The offending employee accepts the help and then continues to do low quality work. Finally, the sensitive supervisor gets irritated and hurt. They are happy to fire the person.

The belligerent supervisor has a very hard time firing anyone. They seem to worry quite a bit about the person bringing legal action or physical force against them. They go through many, many gyrations to try to avoid the firing. They make multi-step disciplinary programs, they work with the person and proclaim that they are "improving" and they even mislead themselves and say "this is really OK". The belligerent supervisor has to get some assistance to do the final push out the door.

The regal supervisor has the least problem with firing employees. They are relieved to remove the threat of the employee to their position.

CHAPTER 14...GRACEFUL ENDINGS

A Story About Resignation Reasons

Ned had been employed for four months. He was well qualified for the position which he had and did an excellent job. He took part in all of the extra company activities and programs. Everyone liked him. His wife's father became ill. He and his wife traveled to be with the father. Ned seemed less content with his job, but still was very dedicated. One day Ned told John that he was resigning. He said that it was because of his wife's father. It was going to be a long illness and they had to move closer to home. John explained these reasons to Ned's supervisors. The supervisors wanted to hang on to Ned, and so Horace decided to speak with him:

"I heard that you are resigning."

Ned sighed:

"Yes, I am. Your management of the projects is so poor that I could not take it anymore."

Horace was taken aback. He was sure that Ned was resigning because of personal reasons. Yet, Ned was saying that he, Horace, was really the problem. Horace repeated the conversation to his other group members. Two other members of the group decided that even if Ned disliked Horace, he was still a good employee, perhaps they could talk with him and convince him to continue working part-time. They said:

"I heard you were unhappy with Horace's management."

Ned replied:

"No, Horace is an OK person. I am leaving because you have done such a poor job of managing the company sales."

All staff members began to look forward to Ned's last day.

Resignations Are Emotional

Firing is not the most common way in which business relationships end. More frequently the association ends because an employee resigns. Resignations upset a static balance which the supervisor is always trying to create. The supervisor hires each employee with an unspoken plan that they will be trained relatively quickly, and then will stay at the same job doing the same work for the next thirty years. The plan also includes the supervisor being a good supervisor and the employee liking them.

When a person resigns the supervisor is angry that their plan is upset and a little worried that the employee is resigning because they do not like the supervisor. The supervisor spends quite a bit of time obsessing about the reasons for the resignation. They become angry with this person for upsetting the balance of things and causing them to have to go through the interviewing, hiring and training process again. During their upset mode, they often ask the employee why they are resigning. This only adds to their misery because the resigning employee rarely gives the real reason that they are leaving. Sometimes the resigning employee does not even understand their reasons themselves.

Employment is not a static thing. People and businesses change in their needs and goals. Employment relationships are more like two gentle streams passing by each other. They intersect with one another for a time and then part again.

Once a supervisor has learned to supervise well, they must come to accept that their time with their employee will not last forever. They must structure their expectations to match this. They must put their energy into training their employee, but not into training them to become a son or daughter to them and carry on the "family line". This is not a life contract, but rather a temporary relationship. Train the employee, teach them, encourage them to better themselves, and know that they will not stay forever. Treat new hiring relationships as continuing new adventures.

When it comes time for the employee to move on, the supervisor can assist them in doing it in a graceful and mature manner.

A Story About a Bad Ending

Ruth had worked hard at her job and was often frustrated with her supervisor. Her supervisor was often frustrated with Ruth. He felt that she should not keep trying to change things, she should just maintain the status quo. Ruth was preparing to resign, as her life-partner had accepted a job in another state. Ruth decided that she could use her leaving to get rid of some of her frustrations with her job. She and her supervisor were in the middle of one of their weekly heated discussions when Ruth said:

"It doesn't matter, because I am resigning, my last day will be April 21."

Her supervisor knew that she was really resigning because of her life-partner, but nonetheless he was startled. Throughout the leaving process, Ruth was professional, but that announcement of her resignation was always hanging there. Ruth felt somewhat proud of the reaction it caused and related it to many people over the years. She felt that it followed the "assertive person" description, she had "won the battle".

One day, 13 years later, Ruth was filling out her application to Law School. The application required a letter of recommendation from a former supervisor or professor. Since Ruth owned her own business, she had no supervisor. The only person Ruth could use was the very person to whom she had made her dramatic leaving statement. Luckily, her former supervisor was more mature than Ruth was at the time, and he made no mention of it when she called him. He happily provided a letter for her. Ruth was lucky.

Analysis: Do Not Burn Bridges

No one knows what the future holds, so it is best to end business relationships as non-emotionally and professionally as is possible. You may say something rude to a resigning employee, and several years later find that they have the final approval on your mortgage application, or worse yet, they are supervising the position that you have just been hired into.

Firing a Person Who Resigns

Some companies immediately fire a person who gives a two-week resignation notice. They claim that this is so that the person will not have an opportunity to copy sensitive material. If the person had an ounce of sense, they would have copied the material long before they tendered their resignation. In reality, the company fires the person because their feelings have been hurt, they feel rejected, and they want to "get even".

A Story About Cindy's Departure

Cindy had found a new job and was pretty excited about it. She wrote a resignation letter and presented it to her supervisor. She said that she was resigning because she had found a better paying job, but that she would work for two weeks from the date of the letter.

Cindy's job required occasional trips out of town. One of the trips was scheduled for the first of her final two weeks. Cindy went to her supervisor and told him that she did not want to go out of town. She would rather spend her time cleaning her office. Her supervisor told her that she had to go out of town. She had to assist in training her replacement who would be traveling with her. Cindy went, grudgingly. The next Monday was the company's regular monthly training. Cindy did not attend. When questioned by her supervisor she explained:

"Since this is my last week, I didn't need to attend."

By the time that Cindy's last day arrived, her supervisor was very irritated with her. At noon he checked to see if she had finished up her last report. She had not. She said:

"I know it is due, but Adam can finish it up next week."

Cindy's supervisor was so irritated he told her to just leave early that day.

Analysis: Assisting in a Graceful Leaving

Once a person has resigned, they often decide that company rules no longer apply to them. They decide not to attend meetings, they come in late and leave early. The supervisor needs to make sure the person who resigns is aware that all rules still apply to them, and the supervisor should define what specific tasks should be completed before they make their final departure. The person who leaves needs to make sure they are remembered as a hard worker up until the end.

A Story About a Successful Return

Belinda liked her job. Her life-partner did not like Belinda's job because at times it required her to work late into the evenings. Belinda's life-partner convinced her to take another job which would have a more predictable schedule. Belinda resigned, and felt very badly about it. She started her new job. She really disliked the job. It did not challenge her at all. Finally she was so depressed that she and her life-partner had a long talk. Her life-partner finally understood what Belinda's original job meant to her. Together they decided that Belinda should check to see if she could get her job back.

Her former supervisor was happy to see Belinda, and gave her her job back. Belinda worked happily at the company for many more years.

A Story About an Unsuccessful Return

Lucy was a good worker. Any job which was assigned to her got done on time. Lucy had some problems with her supervisor. She tried to adapt, but each time her supervisor told her what work to do next, she got irritated. Lucy finally decided to quit. Lucy immediately got a new job, and found that the supervisor at that job was worse. Lucy asked to come back to the first job and was taken back. Within a few months, she resigned again.

Analysis: Should You Take Them Back?

Re-hiring employees who have resigned is a sticky problem. Sometimes it works and sometimes it does not. One of the problems is that, as time goes on, we all tend to forget the bad things and remember the good ones. It is easy to remember the good doughnuts and warm feelings in the coffee room. It is harder to remember the feelings of frustration and inadequacy which force a person to decide to resign. As soon as the situation is re-created, both sides remember the problems. Generally, if a person resigns because of irritation with the company or supervisor, and they are hired back, they will resign again.

The Three Supervisors and Endings

The sensitive supervisor tends to have major feelings of rejection when an employee resigns. They allow the employee to "goof off" for the last few weeks.

The belligerent supervisor gets angry that someone is resigning, and wants to fire them immediately. They have trouble even having a conversation with the person during the last weeks.

The regal supervisor is actually pretty pleased that the person is leaving and may tend to rejoice too much in front of other staff members.

SUMMARY OF BOOK THREE

- The sensitive supervisor is afraid of confrontations.

- The belligerent supervisor wants to yell first and ask questions later.

- The regal supervisor is afraid of losing their job.

HIRING

- Screening potential employees is necessary.

- You need to have a clear idea of the skills and attitudes that you are looking for.

- Know the laws that you are dealing with.

- Your advertisement should fit the job description, not the job benefits.

- When reading resumes, you are looking for 100% failure points.

- Interview questions should deal with skills and attitudes, not personal life issues.

- The interview process is looking for 100% failure points.

- The interviewee should be treated as a guest.

- The hiring decision is difficult to make.

- The job offer is your first supervisor-employee interchange.

- Orientation is necessary.

Book Three Summary Cont'd

FIRING

- Some performance problems are not caused by an employee being bad.

- Some performance problems can be fixed.

- A person who has been given a chance, and not made an effort to improve, should be fired.

- A resigning employee should be helped to leave gracefully.

TAMING YOUR INNER SUPERVISOR: SUMMARY

Book One: Taming

Know yourself
Look to yourself
Think about your people
Think before you speak

Book Two: Day to Day Supervising

Always ask
Your employees cannot be your
   best friends
Communicate
Train
Do not accept failure

Book Three: Hiring and Firing

Hire carefully
Fire carefully
Be polite

INDEX

A

Advertising the job, 14
Attachments (to resume), 20

B

Bad reasons to fire someone, 62
Belligerent supervisor
   defined, 2
   firing, 64
   job endings, 71
   job offers, 41

C

Contracts (employment), 12

E

Employment at will, 11
Employment law, 10-12
Emotions and resignations, 66

F

Firing a person who resigns, 68-69

G

Good reasons to fire, 61

H

Hiring decisions, 35-38
Hiring goals, 6-8
How to fire (summary), 63

I

Interviews are a good thing, 4
Interview questions, 22-26
Interviewee as a guest, 34

N

Negotiations, 41

O

100% failure points, 17, 37
Orientation, 43-44

P

Performance problems, 45-50
Problem employee warning signs, 52

R

Reference checks, 30-32
Regal
    defined, 2
    firings, 64
    job endings, 72
    job offers, 41

S

Screening, 3
Sensitive
    defined, 1
    firing, 64
    job endings, 71
    job offers, 40
Story About
    Attachments (resumes), 19
    Anxious Owner, 45
    Bad Employee, 51
    Bad Ending, 67
    Bad Job Offer, 39
    Better Ad, 15
    Better Firing, 56
    Bob's First Day of Work, 42
    Cindy's Departure, 69
    Delivery (resume), 17
    Easy Decisions (resume), 16
    Firing, 53
    Good Interview, 33
    Good Job Offer, 39

Story About Cont'd
    Hiring Decision, 35
    Interview, 6
    Interview in 1975, 22
    Irate Employee, 9
    Jim's Hiring System, 3
    Long Term Worker, 46
    Money, 32
    New Employee at Haag Environmental Co., 43
    Particular Homemaker, 13
    Performance Problem, 48
    Reference Check, 30
    Resignation Reasons, 65
    Some Past Work Experiences, 29
    Stationery (resume), 18
    Successful Return, 70
    Ted's First Interview, 27
    Unsuccessful Return, 71

U

Unions, 12